TOP 10 MOMENTS IN FOOTBALL

BY NATHAN SOMMER

Minneapolis, Minnesota

Credits

Cover and title page, © Tom DiPace/Associated Press and © Brocreative/Adobe Stock and © razihusin/Adobe Stock; 4, © Eugene__Onischenko/Adobe Stock and © efks/Adobe Stock and © Layn/Adobe Stock and © razihusin/Adobe Stock and © Leonid Yastremskiy/Adobe Stock and © Sirena Designs /Adobe Stock and © Joe/Adobe Stock and © wavebreak3/Adobe Stock and © shock/Adobe Stock and © Andrew Lipovsky/Adobe Stock and © moodboard/Adobe Stock and © Julianna Olah/Adobe Stock and © Hasselblad H6D/Adobe Stock and © Mike Watson Images Limited./Adobe Stock and © digitalskillet1/Adobe Stock and © 103tnn/Adobe Stock and © zphoto83/Adobe Stock; 5, © Icon Sportswire/Getty Images; 6, © UPI/Alamy Stock Photo; 7, © Icon Sportswire/Getty Images; 8, © Associated Press; 8–9, © Sports Illustrated/Getty Images; 10–11, © Focus On Sport/Getty Images; 11T, © Rick Stewart/Getty Images; 12, © Sports Illustrated/Getty Images; 13, © Allen Kee/Getty Images; 14, © Focus On Sport/Getty Images; 15, © Mike Ehrmann/Getty Images; 16, © Andy Lyons/Getty Images; 16–17, © Damian Strohmeyer/Getty Images; 18–19, © Sports Illustrated/Getty Images; 19T, © Panoramic Images/Alamy Stock Photo; 20, © Bettmann Archive/Getty Images; 20–21, © Harry Cabluck/Associated Press; 22TR, © Associated Press; 22ML, © Sipa USA/Alamy Stock Photo; 22BR, © Sports Illustrated/Getty Images; 23BR, © Bombaert Patrick/Adobe Stock

Bearport Publishing Company Product Development Team

Publisher: Jen Jenson; Director of Product Development: Spencer Brinker; Editorial Director: Allison Juda; Editor: Cole Nelson; Editor: Tiana Tran; Production Editor: Naomi Reich; Art Director: Kim Jones; Designer: Kayla Eggert; Designer: Steve Scheluchin; Production Specialist: Owen Hamlin

Statement on Usage of Generative Artificial Intelligence

Bearport Publishing remains committed to publishing high-quality nonfiction books. Therefore, we restrict the use of generative AI to ensure accuracy of all text and visual components pertaining to a book's subject. See BearportPublishing.com for details.

Library of Congress Cataloging-in-Publication Data

Names: Sommer, Nathan, author.
Title: Top 10 moments in football / by Nathan Sommer.
Other titles: Top ten moments in football
Description: Minneapolis, MN : Bearport Publishing Company, 2026. | Series:
    Top 10 sports extremes | Includes bibliographical references and index.
    | Audience term: juvenile
Identifiers: LCCN 2025001524 (print) | LCCN 2025001525 (ebook) | ISBN
    9798895770634 (library binding) | ISBN 9798895775103 (paperback) | ISBN
    9798895771808 (ebook)
Subjects: LCSH: Football--United States--History--Juvenile literature. |
    National Football League--History--Juvenile literature.
Classification: LCC GV955.5.N35 S66 2026 (print) | LCC GV955.5.N35
    (ebook) | DDC 796.332/640973--dc23/eng/20250219
LC record available at https://lccn.loc.gov/2025001524
LC ebook record available at https://lccn.loc.gov/2025001525

Copyright © 2026 Bearport Publishing Company. All rights reserved. No part of this publication may be reproduced in whole or in part, stored in any retrieval system, or transmitted in any form or by any means, electronic, mechanical, photocopying, recording, or otherwise, without written permission from the publisher. Bearport Publishing is a division of FlutterBee Education Group.

For more information, write to Bearport Publishing, 3500 American Blvd W, Suite 150, Bloomington, MN 55431.

CONTENTS

America's Game 4

#10 The Minneapolis Miracle 5

#9 The Philly Special 6

#8 The Ice Bowl 8

#7 Super Bowl XXV 10

#6 The Catch 12

#5 Music City Miracle 13

#4 Super Bowl LI Comeback 14

#3 The Helmet Catch 16

#2 Miami Undefeated! 18

#1 The Immaculate Reception 20

Even More Extreme Football Moments 22

Glossary 23

Index 24

Read More 24

Learn More Online 24

About the Author 24

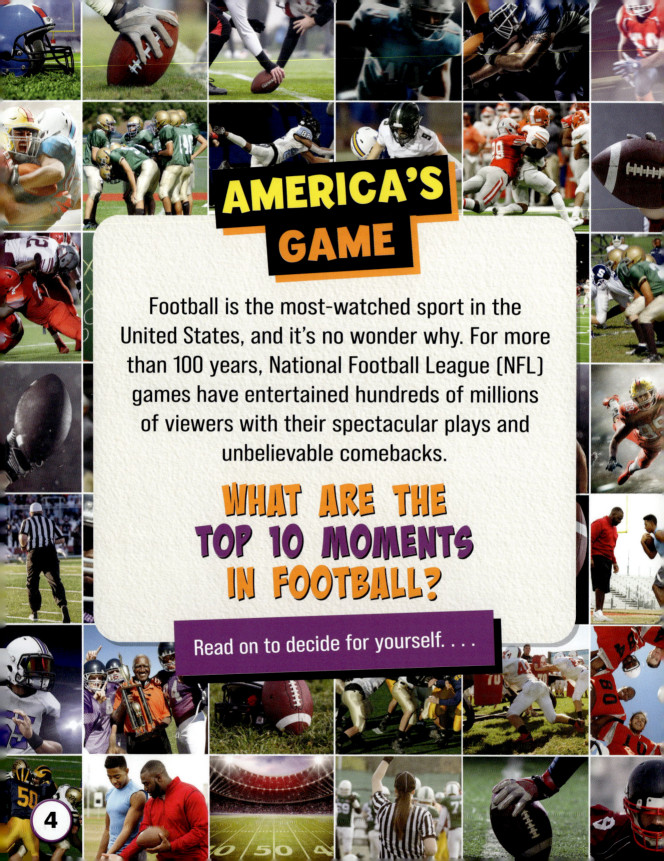

AMERICA'S GAME

Football is the most-watched sport in the United States, and it's no wonder why. For more than 100 years, National Football League (NFL) games have entertained hundreds of millions of viewers with their spectacular plays and unbelievable comebacks.

WHAT ARE THE TOP 10 MOMENTS IN FOOTBALL?

Read on to decide for yourself. . . .

#10 THE MINNEAPOLIS MIRACLE

January 14, 2018 • U.S. Bank Stadium • Minneapolis, Minnesota

As time ticked down during the 2017 **playoff** game between the Minnesota Vikings and New Orleans Saints, the Vikings were down 24–23. With only 10 seconds left, Vikings quarterback Case Keenum threw a 27-yard (25-m) pass to wide receiver Stefon Diggs. Diggs dodged a tackle to make the catch and ran in to score a 61-yd. (56-m) touchdown!

This was the first playoff game to end with a touchdown just before time ran out.

Diggs (#14) scores a touchdown.

After the playoffs, the Vikings advanced to the 2017 NFC Championships.

Keenum had entered the season as the backup quarterback for the Vikings.

#9 THE PHILLY SPECIAL

February 4, 2018 ▪ U.S. Bank Stadium ▪ Minneapolis, Minnesota

Quarterbacks usually throw touchdowns. But during Super Bowl LII, Philadelphia Eagles quarterback Nick Foles caught one! At the end of the second quarter, **center** Jason Kelce snapped the ball to running back Corey Clement. Clement then pitched the ball to **tight end** Trey Burton, who threw a touchdown to a wide-open Foles.

Foles was voted MVP for Super Bowl LII.

Foles was the first player to both throw and catch a touchdown during a Super Bowl.

This was the Eagles' first Super Bowl win.

This **trick play** happened on a fourth down. This is when teams usually attempt field goals.

#8 THE ICE BOWL

December 31, 1967 • Lambeau Field • Green Bay, Wisconsin

The 1967 NFL Championship game was the coldest in league history. In the 4th quarter, the Dallas Cowboys were leading 17–14. But the Green Bay Packers stood less than a yard from the end zone. They could tie the game with a field goal. Instead, quarterback Bart Starr ran the ball down the icy turf to score a game-winning touchdown!

Despite the cold, more than 50,000 fans attended the game.

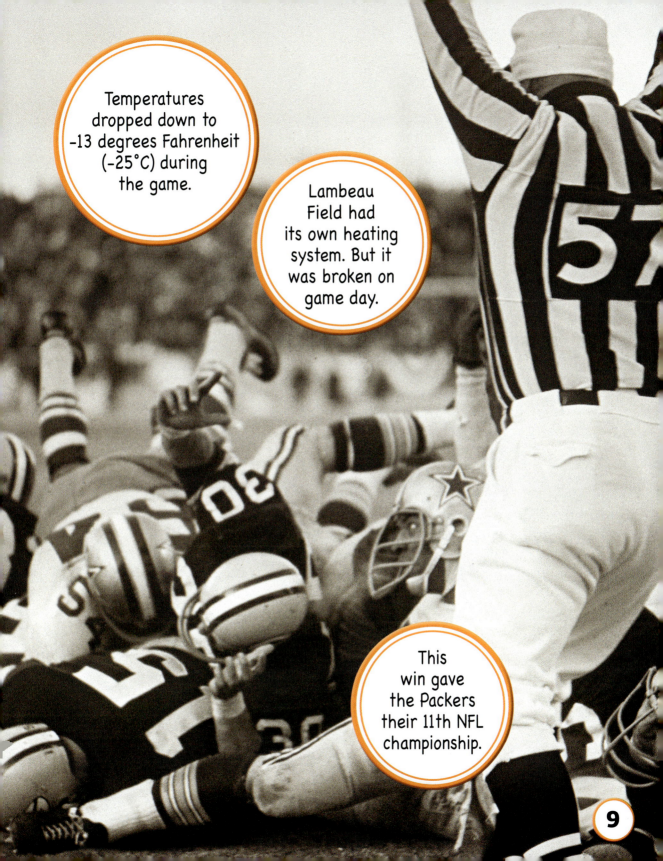

Temperatures dropped down to -13 degrees Fahrenheit (-25°C) during the game.

Lambeau Field had its own heating system. But it was broken on game day.

This win gave the Packers their 11th NFL championship.

#7 SUPER BOWL XXV

January 27, 1991 ▪ Tampa Stadium ▪ Tampa, Florida

Super Bowl XXV pitted the Buffalo Bills' top offense against the New York Giants' top defense. With only 8 seconds left, the Bills were behind 20–19. Bills kicker Scott Norwood set up for what could have been a game-winning field goal. But he missed! The game ended with the Giants celebrating their second Super Bowl win.

This was the only Super Bowl decided by just one point.

Neither team had a **turnover** during the game.

The Bills lost the next three Super Bowls in a row.

Norwood (#11) misses the field goal.

The Giants had entered this game as the **underdogs**.

This was the first Super Bowl ever played by teams from the same state.

#6 THE CATCH

January 10, 1982 • Candlestick Park • San Francisco, California

The 1981 NFC Championships ended with an amazing catch. The San Francisco 49ers were behind the Dallas Cowboys 27–21. San Francisco quarterback Joe Montana was looking to pass while avoiding being **sacked**. Suddenly, Montana saw wide receiver Dwight Clark free at the back of the end zone and threw the ball! Clark's amazing catch won the 49ers the championship!

Clark (#87) catches the ball.

The 49ers won Super Bowl XVI this same season.

Clark's catch is thought of as one of the greatest in NFL history.

Montana has thrown the most touchdowns in 49ers history.

#5 MUSIC CITY MIRACLE

January 8, 2000 ▪ Adelphia Coliseum ▪ Nashville, Tennessee

One of the best **special teams** plays occurred during a 1999 **Wild Card game**. The Buffalo Bills were leading the Tennessee Titans 16–15. With only 16 seconds left, Titans Lorenzo Neal caught a short kickoff. He handed the ball backward to Frank Wycheck, who then threw a **lateral pass** to Kevin Dyson. Dyson ran for a 75-yd. (69-m) touchdown!

This was Dyson's first-ever kickoff return touchdown.

The Titans practiced this play every week leading up to the January 8 game.

Titans coach Alan Lowry created this play 18 years before using it.

#4 SUPER BOWL LI COMEBACK

February 5, 2017 • NRG Stadium • Houston, Texas

The Atlanta Falcons led the New England Patriots 28–3 during Super Bowl LI. But then, the Patriots scored 25 points in a row to tie the game! In overtime, Patriots quarterback Tom Brady drove his team 75 yds. (69 m) downfield. Running back James White later scored a 2-yd. (1.8-m) touchdown. The Patriots won 34–28!

During the game, White caught 14 passes, the most receptions ever in a Super Bowl.

The Patriots' turnaround was the biggest comeback in Super Bowl history.

This was the first Super Bowl to go into overtime.

Before Super Bowl LI, no team had made a comeback after being behind by more than 10 points.

Tom Brady has won seven Super Bowls. This is the most of any player in NFL history.

#3 THE HELMET CATCH

February 3, 2008 • University of Phoenix Stadium • Glendale, Arizona

The New England Patriots were favored to win Super Bowl XLII. They led the New York Giants 14–10. With little time left, Giants quarterback Eli Manning avoided being sacked by three Patriots before **lobbing** a pass to wide receiver David Tyree. Tyree caught the ball—against his helmet! The game later ended with the Giants' win.

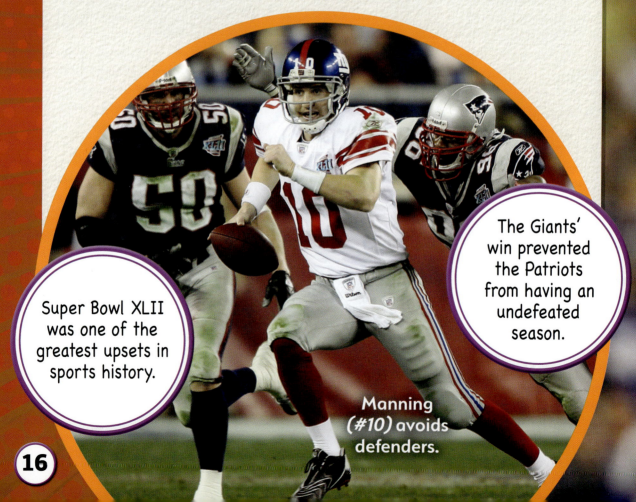

Super Bowl XLII was one of the greatest upsets in sports history.

The Giants' win prevented the Patriots from having an undefeated season.

Manning (#10) avoids defenders.

#2 MIAMI UNDEFEATED!

January 14, 1973 • Los Angeles Memorial Coliseum
Los Angeles, California

The 1972 Miami Dolphins are known as one of the strongest teams in sports history. During Super Bowl VII, head coach Don Shula led his team to victory against the Washington Commanders (known then as the Washington Redskins). The Dolphins ended the season with a 17–0 record. They were the first and only team in the NFL to ever go undefeated!

In 1972, the Dolphins led the NFL in both offense and defense.

Fans and players carrying coach Don Shula

The Pro Football Hall of Fame in Canton, Ohio

Eight members of the 1972 Dolphins became Hall of Famers.

Despite their undefeated season, the Dolphins entered Super Bowl VII as the underdog.

The Dolphins were the first team to have two players rush for more than 1,000 yds. (914 m) in one season.

19

#1 THE IMMACULATE RECEPTION

December 23, 1972 • Three Rivers Stadium • Pittsburgh, Pennsylvania

The Pittsburgh Steelers were running out of time against the Oakland Raiders in the 1972 divisional game. With only seconds left, Steelers quarterback Terry Bradshaw threw a **Hail Mary pass**. The ball hit another player and then flew backward into the arms of Steeler Franco Harris! Harris ran in the catch for the game-winning touchdown.

After the catch, some people say it took 15 minutes to clear cheering fans from the field.

Harris (#32) surrounded by fans

EVEN MORE
EXTREME FOOTBALL MOMENTS

The explosive action of NFL games can create all kinds of extreme moments. Here are some other top moments in football history.

THE ORIGINAL HAIL MARY
In 1975, Dallas Cowboys quarterback Roger Staubach threw a 50-yd. (46-m) pass to receiver Drew Pearson for a touchdown in the final seconds of a game.

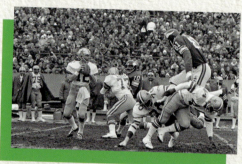

THE LARGEST COMEBACK
At halftime during a game on December 17, 2022, The Minnesota Vikings were behind the Indianapolis Colts 33–0. But the Vikings made the biggest comeback in NFL history to win 39–36 in overtime!

THE HELICOPTER DIVE
Denver Broncos quarterback John Elway jumped headfirst trying to reach a first down during Super Bowl XXXII. As he dove, he bumped into many defenders. This made his body spin like a helicopter!

GLOSSARY

center a player who snaps the ball to the quarterback at the beginning of each play

Hail Mary pass a long forward pass that has a very small chance of being caught

lateral pass a pass thrown sideways or backward to another teammate

lobbing throwing the ball so it travels high and moves slowly

playoff a game in which the winners advance to the conference championship

sacked tackled the quarterback for a loss of yards

special teams players who are on the field during kicking plays

tight end an offensive player who can both block defenders and catch the ball

trick play an unexpected play that tries to fool or catch the opponent by surprise

turnover a play where the offense loses possession of the ball due to a fumble or an interception

underdogs athletes or teams that are not expected to win

Wild Card game a first-round game in the NFL playoffs, played by teams that did not win their division

INDEX

center 6
coach 13, 18
halftime 22
Hall of Fame 19
kicker 10
MVP 6
NFC 5, 12
NFL 4, 8–9, 12, 15, 17–18, 22
overtime 14–15, 22
playoffs 5, 21
quarterbacks 5–6, 8, 12, 14, 16, 20, 22
Super Bowl 6–7, 10–12, 14–16, 18–19, 22
tight ends 6
touchdowns 5–8, 12–14, 20, 22
wide receivers 5, 12, 16

READ MORE

Leed, Percy. *Pro Football by the Numbers (Ultimate Sports Stats).* Minneapolis: Lerner Publications, 2025.

Silverman, Drew. *Great Super Bowl Traditions (NFL at a Glance).* Mankato, MN: Black Rabbit Books, 2025.

LEARN MORE ONLINE

1. Go to **FactSurfer.com** or scan the QR code below.
2. Enter "**10 Football Moments**" into the search box.
3. Click on the cover of this book to see a list of websites.

ABOUT THE AUTHOR

Nathan Sommer graduated from the University of Minnesota with degrees in journalism and political science. He lives in Minneapolis, Minnesota, and enjoys camping, hiking, and writing in his free time.